UNSTUCK

Creating Your Bounce Back Effect

Dr. Jozelle M. Miller

ISBN: ISBN: 978-1-948777-25-4

TABLE OF CONTENTS

DEDICATION

This book is dedicated to my loving Parents the Late Mr. Albert Miller and Reverend Dr. Cynthia Miller.

To

My Father

For the support and encouragement, you showed and for teaching me the value of hard work and staying committed to the fulfillment of my goals.

To

My Mother

For being my inspiration and role model; for teaching me true strength and resilience amidst the hardships of life. I thank you for being my spiritual guide and for teaching me the value and benefits of serving God.

I love and miss you both each day. Continue to sleep in eternal peace.

CHAPTER ONE

MENTAL BATTLEFIELD: FEAR

Can anyone ever truly prepare for all that life has in store for us? For every throw or curveball? For every wave or current in the not-so-distant distance?

A recurring theme in my life has been the uncomfortable sensation of drowning. Feeling that all-consuming and looming fear that life will pull me under and render me completely useless at the mercy of its strength and submergence.

All too often in life, it feels like those waves are right upon me, coming fast and from every direction. I'm right in the eye and heart of the hurricane. Both my heart and mind are screaming at one another ... the notorious game of tug-of-war between emotion and logic that every honest human will admit they know all too well.

My heart is wailing.

I'm drowning.

Logic is trying to throw me a lifeline. A life vest. A rescue boat.

Something.

Anything.

But the all-too-elusive rationality brushes against my struggling fingertips and manages to float upwards as I sink. My yelling and squealing continues. I thrash as it fades in the epitome of deep blue and tiny clear bubbles.

Some anchored, small voice whispers, "You are fine. Just breathe."

But we all know breathing underwater is for mythical mermaids, not mere humans. I can think of a million life experiences when I felt worn down by the rough seas. Haggard. Uncertain. More of a flattened pebble than a human being.

However, up to this point, I have made it through each and every crashing wave and clanging cymbal by the grace of God. Prayers to Him became the undying lyrics to my heart's song. He is the answer. Singing to Him became my every breath. Not by fear, but by trust in the grace and faithfulness of God.

Trust is the secret. Trust is the key. Trust is how I continue to find strength outside myself. Trust is how I "breathe" underwater.

My life is no different from many. Born in the Caribbean on the small island of St. Vincent and the Grenadines, I was a child of two parents. Just your typical nuclear family structure.

My parents worked long and hard days and nights to put food on the table for my sister and me to grant us the amenities needed for a comfortable life.

Don't let me explain it as if it was easy.

You see, I was a sickly child, frail in body due to my lack of appetite. Doctors claimed repeatedly that if I kept going the way I was, I'd die. I was constantly down and out with any sickness that could come to your mind. Common cold? Check. Allergies? Check. Tonsillitis? Check. Sinusitis? Yep, you're getting the hang of it: check, check. I was going through illnesses faster than my peers were going through their favorite cereal boxes.

As many child issues do, this led to my all-knowing Grandmother's advice. Not to me directly, of course, but to my mother. As you must know, nobody knows sickness better than a mother. And, as I'm sure you've also experienced, nobody knows how to cure it quite like they do, either. Or, at least they're fully convinced that they're the only capable ones. It's not their fault, really. It's basically a prerequisite for being a mother. It's as if nurturing is built into their DNA.

"Take the child to the beach. Soak her. Dunk her. The cold will surely drain out."

Spoiler alert: As an obedient daughter herself, my mother listened.She took me to the beach religiously. Every time, she told me to get in. And, as an obedient daughter myself, I listened.

You may be envisioning an enjoyable family excursion detailing the golden glow of the sunset with a faint image of children playing in the water, frolicking with their loving parents...

As much as I'd love to humor the charming visual, I must interrupt your imagination (sorry about that) and let you know that was not at all what took place.

My father dunked me repeatedly underwater. My shrieking did nothing. I can still hear my desperate, yearning screams for my mother, longing for her help—crying for it, actually. Each time, she responded with an echo, hollowness in her voice, "It's okay, baby. You'll feel better."

I went down. Down. And, down again. Underwater. Enclosed. Enveloped. Smushed. Surrounded. Crowded. Cornered. Outnumbered by every water molecule that made up the endless abyss of ever-stretching ocean around me.

Where others may associate the beach with being a safe haven or getaway for refreshment and peace, a great escape, for me, it became my nightmare. The water quickly became my most hated enemy. Number one on my "I Can't Freaking Stand You" list. (Don't worry, I don't have many on that list).

It represented EVERYTHING I feared. Numbness. Monotonous boredom. The unknown. Towering waves. Pitless depth. Endlessness. Nothingness. Total isolation. The deepest, darkest, largest hole that a planet, or person for that matter, can come to know.

Unbeknownst to me, at the ripe age of six years old, the fear and anger I developed towards the beach, or more specifically the thought of drowning, would become my go-to response to any unpleasant experience.

Fight or flight.

The reaction to take flight that, don't get me wrong, was helpful to me as a child in order to protect myself, would later haunt me in adulthood. The same flight mentality would stick around and do me the injustice of under-serving me.

However, as I grew up with the embedded fear of drowning until I couldn't breathe, something else became etched into me alongside it: faith. My mother played two opposing and extreme roles in my life: mother and pastor. Nurturer and judge. Fear and faith. An utterly mysterious—and problematic, if we're being honest—juxtaposition.

The two flip sides of the coin seemed all but inseparable. The grooves, details, edges, and fine lines had all but set in their ways long before she had brought me into this world. However, I couldn't have known that then, so regardless of her history, each emotional jab stung and felt personal.

Often I was the daughter longing for comfort, but she hadn't flipped the mother side of the coin that day. But maybe that's a bit too strong. I would say the result was a young girl desirous of the leniency of a mom but held captive by the strong expectations of a Pastor.

Christian faith was exalted, encouraged, and fortified constantly by who was what I could only piece together as my implanted spiritual navigator. This was just how things were going to be. I was the Pastor's kid, seeking to have the mercy of my mom, but instead my mom was overly concerned about the judgment of the church administration.

It wasn't easy. You may even say I felt like I was drowning as all the pressure to measure up filled my lungs. This period of adolescence marked the second time of my life that the fear of being trapped underwater took hold. The fear wouldn't loosen its metaphorical grip. I feared I'd turn blue, just like the water that plagued me.

Life continued. Or, by life, I mean existing as someone who would reach the expectations of my mom—not myself, but rather a version of myself. An erosion of myself, even. Every edge chipped away by every correction or disapproving eye from my mother, chiseling me into a smooth round pebble again. Maybe the overbearing waters were only pulling me under to wash over me. Maybe the cutting edges of the waves were to sharpen me—I wasn't sure.

The bad thing about pebbles is how small you feel when you're one of them. I lived to make her happy. It wasn't all that bad. I didn't mind, because I loved her so much.

But then I'd get to thinking, you know, the head vs. heart, again. How can I live, truly live, when I am judged constantly? The teenager within me yearned to break free, to join my peers in pleasure, in pain. In messing up, in growing up … but I couldn't.

Christianity did not leave room for desire. Desire was a temptress and I had to sublimate it beyond all costs, or else I'd be denied by my mother or even God.

Yet, out of fear of being denied, I let others deny my sense of self. School fair? No. Pants? No. Ears pierced like other girls? No, at least not until my sister and I finally found the fortitude to break those walls and we heard an ok … Boyfriend? Oh, that one is just hilarious.

Fear of disappointing my mother meant I had to reject my own wanting to fit in when she held strongly that I am to stand out.

Again…

I.

Am.

Drowning.

How can I live up to such perfection?

Was this what God desired or intended for me? Or was it the church, God's people, whose standards were so out of whack and skewed? But questions, like desire, also weren't part of the equation.

Some of the most dangerous moments in history were born during times when questioning wasn't allowed. Yet, it was my reality. But my mom being happy? You just couldn't put a price on that. I would do whatever it took.

If only she could have seen, behind it all, my own longing to be like any other teenager. If only she could have detected my cries for help when I felt disapproved of by my peers. Was I running out of oxygen? If only she could see the bubbles from the surface as I struggled from the depth of water beneath. I was suffering, struggling, strangling from the stifling need to fit in. To be loved. To be seen. To be heard. To be wanted. To connect.

Yet she did not see that side of me; rather she saw a potential deep within me that I had yet to see for myself. She loved me differently from what I naively thought was love. That's what's tricky about water: you could go looking for what's beneath it, but without getting in, your head held high above, looking down, you can only see a reflection of yourself.

I think deep down my mother, like many parents, denied me because she feared I would repeat her own errors, and she fought hard to protect me the best way she knew how.

I kept crying to feel 'normal,' to be like everyone else, but all I could hear was her light, melodic, angelic voice saying, "It's okay baby. God will be pleased with you," just like she said as my dad dunked me below the brim.

Don't get me wrong, my parents taught me a number of valuable lessons that I'd take into adulthood with me. They taught me how to be resolute in my identity. I learned early how to love God, trust God, and build my faith.

They say hindsight is the best kind of vision. As an adult, now I look back at my friends who I naively wanted to follow back when I was denied the opportunity to become a follower. There's some definite value there; a reverberating I have in my heart for the choices my parents made and the lifestyle they stood for. Many still, to this day, sing the praises of my parents and the parenting they imparted my way.

So, was I really drowning? Perhaps not. It's something I definitely mull over and, if I'm honest, often question and doubt.

Even later in life, I stayed the course, choosing Christian principles to guide my life's moral compass. I remember when I started dating seriously towards marriage. I prayed and asked the Lord for a sign that I was making the right choice, and I experienced confirmation.

My mom, the co-captain of my ship even in adulthood, felt confident about my choice. So the plans began. Two and a half years and a marriage (oops) later, my husband decided he no longer wanted to be married ... to me, at least.

This was the pupil of the eye of the hurricane, the peak of the storm, the worst time of my life. Ever. I was thrown around. Dunked. Whipped. Shaken. Crushed. Plunging beneath the water against my will, every single shred of my own strength exhausted. It seemed like my strength meant nothing compared to this aquatic, beastly giant.

"I'm drowning!" I screamed.

It took six months of excruciatingly debilitating emotional and psychological pain before I was brave enough to admit, even just to myself, that my inner screams weren't doing any good if I wasn't letting anyone else hear them.

Ding, ding, ding. Light bulb. Self awareness. Epiphany. "Ah-ha" moment. Whatever you want to call it.

One beautiful Sunday morning, a day I will always be able to vividly recount, I went to church as usual. The metaphorical water had trapped me beneath its grip. Drowning, nearly out of breath, my body somehow found its way to the altar.

The altar call had not even been issued. Yet, there my brave self was. Quite shocking to those around me, I'm sure. But there I was.

She heard my scream this time, as it was not just within.

"MOM! I'M DROWNING!" I screamed with tears in my eyes.

This time, she rushed to my side, quicker than lightning. I collapsed. Weightless. Breathless. Broken and weak. But this time, the mother superseded the pastor as she held me in her arms.

The following day, the man I loved, my husband, officially asked me for a divorce. Our families ripped apart; I wasn't the same. I stepped up above the water that taunted me with fear, and I found my footing. I did not drown; I stood up— bludgeoned, beaten, bruised, bloody. But alive! I realized my body was made to float. I extended my hands and allowed the waves to take me back to safety at the shore.

You see, one of my problems up to that very specific point in my life was showing vulnerability. I never felt comfortable showing my pain to others, and again, leading up to my epiphany moment, I had felt terrified to tell my mother the truth about my marriage—that it was on the rocks, that soon all that would be left was pebbles. Soon I would only have these small, distant memories to hold and roll around in my hands, yet if I got a better look at them, I'd recognize that they were only ruins of something that once was.

I didn't want to be a disappointment to her, an embarrassment or black spot in her ministry. But at that point, I had no more fight in me. No more pretense. So I closed my eyes, exhaled deeply, let go, and began floating in self–reprieve. I don't know how else to word it than I was being carried by the Lord himself at this point, that eye of the hurricane was only the precursor for the biggest wave that was about to come.

Yep, you bet: when it rains, it pours.

Nearly a year later, following that entire ordeal, the tsunami hit. The love of my life, my rock, my support, my fortress, my best friend, my mom, was diagnosed with lung cancer.

D

R

O

W

N

I

N

G

Subsequently, my sweet mother died after battling for eight long months.

I. Am. Drowning.

Who hears us at this point when we go through tribulations THIS large in size? Who hears us at our lowest of lows?

You know when the reality of just how low you feel overwhelms you? I felt like no one, absolutely no one, would hear me or see me. I felt my own life release out of my body. It wasn't dramatic. It had just walked away after shutting the door just as quickly as it had walked up to it, without so much as a word. No light left in its wake.

When I looked up for help from the Lord, I let Him know I am drowning; I let him know how bitter I was. After all, how could He not have heard my mother, who prayed over so many people? I'd watched Him hear her then because I saw them healed. She needed Him, yet He hadn't acted on her or my behalf, and certainly not in the manner I had wanted Him to.

Darkness consumed me. It became my middle name. I had hit the bottom of the sea. I was taking in boat loads of water, but I didn't care to fight at that point.

Just when I thought it was all over, I remember hearing a sermon by Bishop T.D. Jakes:

"What do you do when God says no? When you PRAY and PRAY for a specific answer and He STILL says no?!"

In that moment, I heard the voice of the Lord as clear as day. He was right next to me. He met my scream of "I AM DROWNING," with His response. Romans 8:35-39:

Who shall separate us from the love of Christ?

Shall tribulation or distress or persecution or famine or nakedness or peril or sword?

As it is written for thy sake, we are killed in the day long, all the day long.

We are counted as sheep for the slaughter.

Nay, in all these things we are more than conquerors, through Him that loved us.

For I am persuaded that neither death nor life, nor angels, nor principalities, nor powers, nor things present, nor things to come, nor height, nor depth, nor any other creature shall be able to separate us from the love of God which is in Christ Jesus Our Lord.

If there's one thing I've learned about the Lord, it's that it is in His divinely mysterious nature to strip away every last thing or person who is in competition with Him in your life. He wants your gaze and attention.

I finally reached the point where I saw God more than ever. In order to get back to a safe harbor, I had to acknowledge the presence of God. I had to get over myself for the journey it took me to get here and I had to seek God's forgiveness for my attitude and anger. I needed to declare Him to be God of my situation; I had to float. I was reminded of the song "Ocean" by Hillsong:

You call me out upon the waters

The great unknown where feet may fail

And there, I find You in the mystery,

In oceans deep

My faith will stand

And I will call upon Your name

And keep my eyes above the waves

When oceans rise

My soul will rest in Your embrace

For I am Yours and You are mine

Your grace abounds in deepest waters

Your sovereign hand

Will be my guide

Where my feet may fail and fear surrounds me

You've never failed and You won't start now

So, I will call upon Your name

And keep my eyes above the waves

When oceans rise

My soul will rest in Your embrace

For I (Jozelle) am yours and you are mine

It was at this point that I extended my arms and began floating. I said, "Spirit, lead me where my trust is without borders, let me walk upon the waters wherever you would call me. Take me deeper down than my feet could ever wander and my faith will be made stronger."

There was a quiet period in my life following this. I can equate that to lying on the shore catching my breath. The waves came in and rushed against me, but I was grounded firmly in the sand. But eventually the unpredictability of life kept knocking me over as soon as I stood up. Things got to the point where the waves would appear out of nowhere and knock me over before I could even take a step.

You won't believe what happens next.

This time it was my dad who was diagnosed with cancer and subsequently taken from me.

You know that feeling that you cannot breathe? You try your best to inhale but there simply is no oxygen? No air to be found? I couldn't catch my breath. I knew, on paper, I'm a psychologist, so I recognized this was compound grief. But that knowledge seemed insufficient to help my pain. I had to fight the darkness all over again.

My pillows were drenched and my body mass shredded. Again I screamed, "I am drowning," but this time it wasn't the fear and hopelessness I felt before, It was apprehension and distrust in life.

I waited each day with bated breath, waiting for the inevitable, inescapable shoe to drop. I was drowning from the inside from all of my fear. To exhale would mean to let go, to let down my guard. If I didn't hold it all in, my heart may be vulnerable, and I could lose someone else. And I simply was not prepared to let that happen again. I was barely hanging on.

I remember hearing once that it is not the water surrounding the boat that causes it to sink, but rather the water that gets in. But have you ever started drowning from the inside? How do you let the water out? How do you release excess water flooding your lungs and impeding your ability to breathe?

What typically causes us to feel as if we are drowning amidst challenges? One of the things I became extremely mindful of is that it is not always real. For many of us, the water may not be as treacherous as it appears in our minds. Our imaginations, anxiety, worry, and existential dread can cause a drip to seem like a rushing waterfall. Embedded fear causes us to feel out of control.

It is at that point we have to fact-check: review the situation and examine the evidence that may be around. Pay attention to which things are being amplified by our emotions.

I often have to remind myself to breathe, because when I get anxious or fearful, I hyperventilate, leading to light-headedness. Deep breathing actually sends a message to your brain to slow down and relax. Your heart rate slows and you begin to experience the calm.

There are so many external factors to affect us; there are so many expectations leading us daily. I grew up under the expectation of the church and the perceived expectations of my parents, teachers, and peers. Such intrusion lent itself to losing one's identity. Living to please everyone else is extremely exhausting. Until you fully get to the point of prioritizing your needs and putting yourself first, it will always be a drowning experience.

I remember being so scared about what people in the church would say about my sister and me. My mother spoke about what other people would say about us, how me being good would mean I'd have a better testimony, and so on. While I appreciated the caution, it was suffocating.

I remember the many times I felt as if I were drowning. The one thing that would bring me back to the surface most of the time would be not wanting to cause my family pain. You know when you're that desperate to make someone else happy?

Still, over time I have learned how to be a fighter. To this day, I continue to persevere over the challenges of life. I push through. I breathe. I fight harder. I breathe again.

Drowning is never an option.

I've learned to hold what's in my grasp, things I have control over. I have mastered taking care of those things. The rest, I leave alone. This has been the key to my survival.

During my divorce, I got really ill. Quite a few things were going on in my body, and I ended up having to go to the doctor. After running a battery of tests, it was revealed that I was unable to biologically have kids.

This was a very significant drowning experience for me. The worst part about this time was that I had to endure it all by myself. So many of the people who had been closest to me were gone. All I wanted to do was give up; there was absolutely no light shining on my life from anywhere around me.

My breathing was labored; living and simply breathing felt like a modern-day job. I felt like I was losing all around me; everything was simply disappearing and crumbling all around me.

However, God reminded me that He is a restorer. He is One that would, as we often say in the Caribbean, give you double for your trouble. He took me to Isaiah 43:

When you walk through the fire, you will not be burned;

The flames will not set you ablaze.

For I am the LORD, your God,

The Holy One of Israel,

Your Savior.

As I read that scripture, it really resonated with me. I found comfort that even if I would not be able to biologically have a child, I understood that my love could still be given to others in different ways. There were kids out there who needed love through adoption and fostering. The Lord positioned these opportunities in my life. Being placed on the adoption committee in my country would mean I'd get to help work on teams that decide which families babies would go to.

Humility crashed down around me and reminded me that even though I could not have a baby for myself, I could always help other people. I could always use my own story and experience to relate to those who have gone through similar situations of infertility, miscarriages, or other losses.

Through my position on that committee, I was able to bless others. I believe that God sees my heart and love for others and that one day I'll be able to be blessed as well. Someday it'll be my turn, and the Lord will bless me with a child. The baby will be my double for my trouble, my restoration and redemption.

The time is coming for me to stand on my feet and exhale again. I will not drown.

CHAPTER TWO

GOD'S PROMISES

When we're children, we're taught to trust God, right? To pray and have faith. But when you were a kid, did you feel like you truly understood what that all meant? Can kids have a grasp on the things unseen?

I sure didn't.

With my childhood innocence and naiveté, I thought faith was like some sort of magic formula; it was like believing in the Tooth Fairy, Santa Claus, or even the Easter Bunny. Once a request was made, it would be magically granted because I was a good person, and good things happen to good people.

But as you know, this never lasts. Reality inches closer and closer to us each time we learn a lesson, from childhood to adolescence to adulthood. These lessons start out small, as we too are small. Depending on our upbringings, typically, our confrontations with reality get harsher as we age.

I remember when it dawned on me that prayer didn't work like magic. Having made numerous requests that were either flat-out unfulfilled or not at all in the timing I would have envisioned for myself, I remember my reaction to reality.

I remember asking my mom, "Is God made up like Santa Claus? It doesn't seem like He really listens to my prayers."

I remember her astonishment. Likely functioning first as a pastor instead of a mother, she probably thought, *In what manner of blasphemy can my child have the gumption to ask this question?*

Then, her secondary role as a mom kicked in. She saw my childlike innocence and had empathy instead of blame. She explained the difference between the magical fictional characters and the highest God who lives and reigns.

I learned that prayer was not a matter of asking and expecting immediate answers or results, but rather, understanding the character of God. She taught me that God cannot lie and that He always fulfills the promises He makes.

Through the stories of the Bible, I got to know God more because it showed me what God did and what was important to Him. Through the Bible and also through prayer and worship, I met God for myself, and all that I had learned about Him in the stories became more than just theoretical knowledge; rather, it became a personal experience. I often enjoyed what the songwriter said: "when I think of the goodness of Jesus and all He's done for me, my soul cries out Hallelujah, I Thank God for saving me." I learned early in the game that when you commit your life to God, He leads you through life. When you are His Child and relate to Him as your Heavenly Father, that is the best way to get to know the character of God.

Two of my favorite stories in the Bible are the stories of Job and Joseph. These two stories are the perfect examples of God's faithfulness and the promise that He will never leave or forsake us.

I remember when I read the story of Job for the first time, a thought crept in that this must be some sort of sorcery. How else could it be possible that someone could be so "bad lucky," as we would say in St. Vincent? In other words, I didn't understand how this wasn't too good to be true. I did not perceive Job's life to be a lesson of God's favor; I saw it more so as Job's fate.

So often we are so busy seeing the negatives in situations that we do not take the time to appreciate God's at times quiet but ever-present work behind the scenes. We don't take the time to appreciate that even in the bad times, God is advocating on our behalf and using his will and strength to piece things together in a way that will ultimately be for our best.

As I matured and adulthood crept closer, life began taking its jabs at me. I began to see living and surviving as a day job. I'd sweat and try, punch in my time, wipe my brow, and hop in bed, only to do it all over again the next day. I remember the many times I asked the Lord, "Why me?"

But that's the moment when you have to buckle down. When the tears flow, when the hurt and brokenness close in, when you feel like you can't breathe, that's when you can find the greatest comfort in Him.

So that's exactly what I did. I sought the Holy Spirit who would immediately act as my comfort. I realized that through seeking Him, I'd find I wasn't alone whatsoever. If I focused on all I did not have and lost my sight of Him, of course I would feel lonely.

The endlessly faithful Holy Spirit would show me that whenever I took a long, hard walk against the resistance of a sandy beach, I'd look back and see that the only reason I could only see my own footprints was because I was being carried by my beautiful Savior.

I often use the words of Job from Job 13:15: "Though He slays me, yet will I trust him, but I will surely defend my ways to his face."

I grew to learn that once the Lord has allowed something in your life, He has a bigger plan. Any pain or hard days are unto a beautiful discovery. A Caribbean saying of my people goes like this: "God wouldn't give you more than you can bear, and what is for you can never be un-for you."

This basically means that our lives are chosen for us and everything is for a reason. Once we are walking in the will of God, He will see us through anything. All we have to do is trust. The lesson here is that faith is unwavering trust and belief, an undying, optimistic hope that things will work out as God planned them.

This is undoubtedly mirrored in His promise in 3 John 2: "Beloved, I wish above all things that thou mayest prosper and in health held even as thy soul prospereth."

It is through learning His promises that my faith was built and strengthened.

The main five promises I hold and that I hope to encourage you to also hold, are:

PROMISE #1:

God is always with me; I will not fail.

PROOF:

"He reminds us so we can confidently say the Lord is my helper, I will not fail, what can man do to me?"

(Hebrews 13:6)

PROMISE #2:

God is always in control so I will not doubt.

PROOF:

"But when you ask Him, be sure that your faith is in God alone, do not waver, for a person with divided loyalty is as unsettled as a wave of the sea that is blown and tossed by the wind."

(James 1:6)

PROMISE #3:

God is always good, I will not despair.

PROOF:

"Trust in the Lord, have faith, do not despair, trust in the Lord."

(Psalms 27:14)

PROMISE #4:

God is always watching, I will not falter.

PROOF:

"If you falter in times of trouble, then how small is your strength?"

(Proverbs 24:10)

PROMISE #5:

God is always victorious, I will not fail.

PROOF:

"God is within her, she will not fall, God will help her at the break of day."

(Psalms 46:5)

I can't pretend for a second that it has always been easy. I had to learn to constantly keep my mind in the right place. I know now why the Bible said that we are to renew our minds daily; the devil knows that our minds will always be the battlefield.

MENTAL BATTLEFIELD: REWIRING

This is where years of psychological practice comes in. Here are my go-to tips; I hope my own lessons can help serve you and save you further time. That would make each of the hard days I've had worth it.

MIND TIP #1:

Start the day with positive affirmations and prayer.

REASON:

How you start the morning sets the tone for the rest of the day. Have you ever woken up on the wrong side of the bed, and then, even worse, it feels like nothing good happens for the rest of that day? This usually happens when we start the day with a negative emotion and bring that pessimistic energy with us into the rest of the day. This sets each experience we'll have up for failure, almost a self-fulfilling prophecy.

APPLICATION:

Instead of letting this dominate you, start your day with prayer. Prayer can be done in so many different ways than just bending a knee with your hands together and head bowed! Prayer can be a flow from your heart and life, an energy of worship from inside out.

Be thankful and say a positive affirmation over your life. Talk to yourself in the mirror. Even if you feel silly, smile and laugh with yourself in reckless abandon; finding joy in the freedom to be the person beloved by God—who you were created to be.

Speak statements like "Today will be a good day," or "I am going to be awesome today."

You will be AMAZED by how much your words

help to improve your day, and even beyond that, your thoughts! Your thoughts are powerful and have the ability to change your attitude and actions, which ultimately can shape the life around you. "Fake it until you make it," while a much criticized saying, can definitely be a tool for success when used properly. Faking it does not have to mean being inauthentic or deceitful. Be true to who you are, but also, when you feel lousy but want to have a good day, believe beyond how things feel and let your faith fill in the gaps. With God, believing beyond what the eyes can see can fill you with joy beyond your understanding! That's my version of "fake it until you make it."

MIND TIP #2:

Focus on the good things, however small.

REASON:

The small things are the big things, and if you're faithful with what is small, you'll be able to take on more, one step at a time. One scripture I love that reminds me of this is Zachariah 4:10:

"Despise not the day of small beginnings."

We so often wait for the big glamorous events to celebrate or feel good that we end up taking so much for granted. How lifeless does it sound to live for the next big thing, instead of living fully everyday? Yet we all do this constantly—it's almost even ingrained in us to live that way. Taking everything as a blessing gives you intentionality and control over your mood, gratefulness, and spirit. Dare I say it, gratefulness allows you to "take your life back," in a sense, by deeming it all as a blessing from Him.

APPLICATION:

Undoubtedly, we are going to encounter obstacles throughout our days. In fact, there's no such thing as a perfect day. When you encounter challenges, try to focus on the benefits, no matter how slight or unimportant they may seem to you. For example, if you get stuck in traffic, as I often do, think about how you can now use the time to listen to good music, a sermon, or a motivational book. Use the time wisely. Again, be intentional!

MIND TIP #3:

Find humor in bad situations.

REASON:

This is definitely one of my favorite pastimes. I love to laugh and as they say, laughter is the best medicine.

Freeing yourself to laugh constantly takes the pressure off of you to take every little thing about yourself so seriously.

APPLICATION:

Allow yourself to experience humor in even the darkest or most trying situations. Remind yourself that this situation will make for a good story or joke later on in life. Believe me when I tell you, you can actually find a light moment in any situation. Once you are open enough to look for it, you will find it. Don't feel guilty for allowing yourself to be light or happy, either. Sometimes we think we have to punish ourselves. Instead, turn failures into lessons. We are not perfect and oftentimes we push so much for perfection, but we should really be seeking excellence. You're going to make mistakes and experience failures in multiple contexts, at multiple jobs and tasks, and with multiple people.

Instead of focusing on how you have failed, think about what you are going to do next time. Turn your failure into a lesson. Conceptualize this as a concrete rule: failure is your first attempt at learning. You have just figured out that this particular action will not work, so you're going to move on to try something else.

MIND TIP #4:

Transform negative self-talk into positive self-talk.

REASON:

Negative self-talk can creep up easily and is often hard to notice. You might think, *I'm so bad at this*, or *I shouldn't have tried that*, but these thoughts turn into internalized feelings and might cement your conceptions of yourself. This is a dangerous game to play; just as we've discussed positive thinking having enough power to transform your thoughts and environment, negative thoughts can do the same—but for the worse!

APPLICATION:

When you catch yourself doing this, stop and replace those negative messages with positive ones. For instance, a negative thought might come that says, *I am so bad at this*, but you can change that into saying "I am bad at this, but I am going to get better with practice."

You shouldn't confine yourself to a thought process that says that you cannot or that you are less. Instead of having a negative thought and allowing it to have a period at the end and become a fact, ALWAYS turn it around. STOP the negative thoughts. Reframe, reconstruct, and start speaking life about yourself and into your situation.

MIND TIP #5:

Focus on the present.

REASON:

I'm talking about the present. Not just today, not just this hour, but this exact minute. Living presently allows you to be grateful for the here and now instead of reliving your past mistakes or worrying about the future.

APPLICATION:

You might be getting yelled at by a friend, a co-worker, or a boss. In times like this, when anxieties and tensions are high, slow down. Think about it: What in this exact moment is happening that is so bad? Forget the comments he or she has made five minutes ago. Focus on what is happening right now in this individual moment. Most of the time, in most situations, you will find that it is not as bad as you imagine it to be. More sources of negativity stem from a memory of a recent event or the exaggerated imagination of a potential future event. Stay in the present moment. Breathe and ground yourself by focusing on something unchanging, something you can always count on. Maybe that's a photo of your dog, the feeling of your hands as you touch them with your fingertips, or a favorite song.

MIND TIP #6:

Find positive friends, mentors, and family.

REASON:

One of the things I usually say is, "Show me your network, and I will tell you how far you'll go." When you surround yourself with positive people, you'll hear positive outlooks, positive stories, and positive affirmations. Their positive words will sink in and affect your own line of thinking, which then affects your words, and in turn, contributes to the group.

APPLICATION:

Finding positive people to fill up your life can be difficult at times, but you need to eliminate the negativity in your life before it consumes you. Never feel obligated to stay in a space that you have outgrown. Do what you can to improve the positivity of others and let their positivity affect you in the very same way.

Almost anybody in any situation can apply these mind tips to their lives and increase their positive outlook. Trust me, these are foolproof. I drink my own Kool-Aid, which means that these are things that I have tried, and they have worked. Just know that positive thinking offers compounding results and returns, so the more often you practice it, the greater the benefits you will realize.

SPIRITUAL BATTLEFIELD

Practicing all of these may be good, but one must never take it for granted that the enemy, and king of lies, is working overtime to destroy us. Spiritual warfare is real. The things we see occurring in the visible, physical world are directly connected to the invisible spiritual world. The effects of the war going on in the unseen world reveal themselves in our strained and damaged relationships, emotional instability, mental fatigue, physical exhaustion, and many other areas of life.

Many of us feel pinned down by anger, unforgiveness, pride, comparisons, insecurity, discord, or fear. The list can go on and on, but the overall primary nemesis behind all of these outcomes is the devil himself. That's why we are reminded in Ephesians 6:12, "For our battle is not against flesh and blood, but against the rulers, against the authorities, against the world powers of this darkness, against the spiritual forces of evil in the heavens."

It is a must that we seek God for spiritual discernment and wisdom so that we will have a clearer understanding of who we are in Christ and all that comes with that relationship.

THE ARMOR OF GOD

In order to combat the spiritual attacks and to make sure we strengthen our faith, we are to be clothed fully in the armor of God. We are admonished by Paul in Ephesians 6:10-18, to be strong in the Lord and the Power of His might. To put on the armor of God so that we will be able to stand against the devil's schemes.

RESOURCE #1: BELT OF TRUTH

Part of the armor, the belt of Truth, is a belt that holds a believer's armor together. A soldier is only fully ready for battle when he is girded with his belt.

Ultimate truth can be found in God's Word and in the person of Jesus Christ. This truth must be known, in order for us to be protected against our fleshly desires, the allure of the world, and the Father of lies. It is the truth that grounds us and reminds us of our identity in Christ.

In John 14:6 scripture reminds us that, "Jesus is the way and the truth and the life. No one comes to the Father except through him."

APPLICATION:

We are told that we must know this Truth in order to protect ourselves against our flesh, the world, and the father of lies. Truth grounds us and reminds us of our identity in Christ. The world is filled with so many ideologies; we must seek each day to hold on to the absolute truth found in knowing God's direction and ordinances for our lives.

RESOURCE #2: BREASTPLATE OF RIGHTEOUSNESS

The second piece of the armor is the breastplate of righteousness. As believers, we have no righteousness apart from that which has been given us by Christ. The breastplate protects our vital organs; we must choose daily to live a right life rooted in God's word, protecting our heart and defeating the enemy.

APPLICATION:

We must identify righteous activities that can help to strengthen our Christian walk. It is also important that we identify those unrighteous activities that we engage in that work to weaken us. Some of these things can be simply watching TV shows that are not in line with our beliefs, or exposing ourselves to immoral behavior. Each time we open up ourselves to any unrighteous act , we weaken our spiritual safety by granting the Devil unnecessary space in our lives.

RESOURCE #3: SANDALS WITH THE GOSPEL OF PEACE

These sandals were made to help protect the soldier's feet during their march to battle. They had extremely thick soles and wrapped perfectly around their ankles in a way that protected against blisters. As believers, we have peace in knowing we are secure in what Jesus has done for us.

APPLICATION:

We are to share our testimonies with others; this is the easiest and most effective way to share the Gospel. When others hear how Jesus changed our lives, they too will want to meet our wonderful savior. We are to be a living, walking example of God's love; when we carry ourselves with the fruit of the spirit, people will stop and take notice.

RESOURCE #4: SHIELD OF FAITH

We are to put on the shield of faith. Trusting in God's power and protection is imperative in remaining steadfast. When the battle rages, we must remember that God works all things for good for those who love the Lord. He is always true to his promises.

APPLICATION:

When the attacks of the devil come, we are to combat them with the reminders of God's goodness. Focus on the promises of God. In Deuteronomy 31: 6, we are reminded that God will meet all our needs. In Psalm 50:10, scripture reminds us that we can call on him and he will answer. He will make our path in life straight, according to Proverbs 3:5-6.

RESOURCE #5: HELMET OF SALVATION

The believer's helmet is the most crucial piece of the armor. Without the in-dwelling Holy Spirit that enters the believer at the moment of salvation, all other armor is useless. Salvation empowers believers to fight. It protects us in our weakness. Without salvation, we have no victory.

APPLICATION:

In life we will be faced with some dark times, but we are to be comforted in knowing that our salvation will light the way for us through those dark times. There is such a great satisfaction in knowing without a shadow of a doubt that we are going to heaven because of Christ's ultimate sacrifice of love, when he died on the cross.

We are to place our thoughts on things that are heavenly and be intentional in feeding our minds with the word of God.

RESOURCE #6: SWORD OF THE SPIRIT

Then we are to remember the sword of the spirit. Our sword is the Word of God, both the written and the incarnate Word. All other pieces of the soldier's arsenal are defensive weapons, but not his sword. With God's Word, we are truly able to fight and defeat all enemies. Christ used Scripture to defeat Satan when He was tempted in the desert. We must do the same.

APPLICATION:

Every other piece of armor protects us against attacks. Think of prevention instead of actually attacking, for example, taking Vitamin C to prevent a cold, whereas your cells actually fight the cold once you have it.

With God's Word, we are able to truly fight and defeat the enemy. We must know the Word so that we can use the Word as well as prayer, one of the other more important pieces of the armor, against the enemy.

With prayer, we show our reliance upon God to act and move. Our entire armor is rooted in His strength. Without His presence, we are powerless in the fight. We must fight on our knees. The one who has won the war is with us in battle. We will see victory when we fight in His power. It is not by might or power, but by the Spirit of the Lord.

CHAPTER THREE

MENTAL BATTLEFIELD: GRIEF

I believe the most gut-wrenching pain anyone could experience and endure is the death of a loved one. There is absolutely no amount of preparation that makes that moment any less painful or bearable. I grew up fearing the death of my loved ones so badly. It was never a thought I could even slightly entertain because of the physical and mental distress I would experience.

I remember my bowels becoming so weak at the thought. My heart would race and my palms would sweat. It was so bad that I would pray time and time again for the Lord to take my life first. It might sound heroic, but, honestly, it was from a selfish place.

I didn't want to be the one to endure the pain and felt my loved ones would better cope in my absence. They would be able to grieve losing me better than I would be able to grieve losing them.

WHAT IS GRIEF?

So, what the heck is grief anyway? It gets lumped in with loss, depression, trauma, sadness, shock, and so on, but it's important to understand what grief truly is.

Grief is a natural response to loss, the emotional suffering you feel when something or someone you love is taken away from you. Often the pain of loss can feel overwhelming. You may experience all kinds of difficult and unexpected emotions, from shock or anger to disbelief, guilt, and profound sadness. The pain of grief can also disrupt your physical health, making it difficult to sleep, eat, or even think straight, but these are normal reactions to loss, and the more significant the loss to you, the more intense your grief will be. For instance, when my mom died, the grief I felt there superseded what I felt when my father passed away. It was not because I did not love my father, but my connection to my mom was greater and deeper, so her passing affected me more. Additionally, by the time my dad died, I had developed stronger coping mechanisms.

WHAT DOES GRIEF LOOK LIKE FROM THE OUTSIDE?

One thing I have learned is that grief is a highly individualized experience. There is no right or wrong way to deal with grief, but one of the worst things I remember during my grieving process was the encouragement to be strong. What does that really even mean though? I realize that many people, myself included, lack a true understanding of what it means to be strong. Sometimes we think strength is about getting up, working hard, and making things work out for ourselves. We think we need to bury any pain and be all about the hustle, and that not having time for self care is a sign of working hard. But I learned strength isn't about holding back the tears and forgetting our pain.

Strength is actually all about feeling the pain. Strength is crying. Strength is existing in that space but still being resilient enough to find your breath and keep it going.

The bottom line about grieving is that it doesn't look the same for everyone. How you grieve depends on many factors, including your personality, coping style and skills, life experience, faith, and how significant the loss was to you.

It's important to note that the process cannot be rushed. Let me say that again, the process cannot be rushed. It's okay if it takes you six months before you're able to cry, or maybe it takes you six months of crying.

In every family, the grieving process takes time and looks different. Healing happens gradually; it can't be forced or hurried, and there is no normal timetable for grieving. Some people start to feel better in a week, others months, and some even roll on into years. Yet for others, it may even take years before they are able to feel the true weight of it.

Whatever your grieving experience may be, it's important for us to be patient with ourselves and to give us the fairness we deserve in allowing the process to naturally unfold. We deserve that compassion and patience, not just from God and others, but from ourselves.

HOW DOES ONE DEAL WITH GRIEF?

So, how do we deal with the grieving process really? I think I would put on my psychologist hat in responding to that. While grieving a loss is an inevitable part of life, there are different ways we can cope with the pain.

STEP 1: ACKNOWLEDGMENT

First, acknowledge your pain, and understand that you have to feel to heal.

The healing process comes when the pain intensifies. Remember falling down as a child, getting a bruise initially but realizing that as the healing process started the skin became significantly sorer? Nonetheless, as humans, we're comforted in learning that while we feel more pain, we can know that healing has started and relief is on the way.

Accept that grief can trigger many different and unexpected emotions. It can cause irritability and frustration over the most trivial of things. Your grief inside manifests outwardly through your behaviors.

Seek out a few people who care about you that you believe you can handle being face-to-face with even during the intense times. Self-isolation is not helpful when not moderated. It's okay to show your vulnerable side, especially to those who love and care about you.

It was so easy for me to pull away and hide in my house. Living alone became my safe haven, the space where I was allowed to not be okay. I didn't have to put on a smile. In fact, I did not have to do anything that I was not ready to do.

But at the same time, I realized that as I isolated myself and pulled away from others, my grief was prolonged. My grief took residence in my spirit to the extent that it became daunting.

Those you allow into your small, trusted circle during this difficult time should help you rebuild the walls that are crashing down. These roles will not be for the faint of heart and should be your truest, closest, most dependable loved ones who won't turn away when things get tough.

These friends may have to physically pick you up sometimes.

Let them.

These loved ones will help you stack the bricks and rebuild.

Let them.

These friends will be your affirming station, giving

you words of life when all you want is to die. But sometimes this community will need to just be quiet and listen—to be a safe space and haven where nothing needs to happen at all. Don't be afraid to let them know what you need. Like anything, it takes practice, so don't worry if you are not immediately good at this.

STEP 3: PHYSICAL SELF-CARE

It's also important during grief that you support yourself emotionally by taking care of yourself physically. We can't deny our physical needs to eat, sleep, exercise, and take medication. We should not allow the grief to stop our normal functioning. Recognize the difference between grief and depression.

If what you're feeling is totally unbearable, to the point that you've lost interest in any and everything, that you can't find any silver lining or positivity from anything around you, then it is important that you be assessed for clinical depression, which can develop as a result of a stressor.

THE FIVE STAGES OF GRIEF

I learned the five stages of grief to the extent that they were embedded inside of me. They are:

Denial -> Anger -> Bargaining -> Depression -> Acceptance

Each individual must be allowed to go through the grieving process on their own terms for themselves. Know that it's okay if your process is messy and not linear. No one jumps from one stage to the next in perfect order and it's okay to jump around and evolve. The stages of grief reveal themselves on an individual basis.

DENIAL

When it comes to denial, I remember that I kept saying and thinking, "This can't be happening to me," when I was going through the losses of both of my parents. *This can't be. I'm still grieving losing my Mom and now I'm losing my Dad, too. This can't be.*

Even with my marriage, I kept saying maybe he's really not cheating. Maybe this, maybe that. My mind would create its own defense as a coping mechanism so that I'd be able to self-soothe, to ease my own pain by saying that this particular thing may not really exist.

ANGER

I kept asking, "Who is to be blamed for all of this?" When my Mom died, I blamed God. I got to a really low point where I felt that God betrayed me and disappointed me because He didn't heal my mom. But I later understood that God is always present, even when the outcome is not what we want.

BARGAINING

If I only told you the number of times I tried to bargain with God to say that if You do this then I'll do that!

DEPRESSION

Then we have Depression. To start or to do anything, you have this feeling of doubt and tiredness you can't shake. Scientifically, your brain is in a constant state of fog that makes everything harder to do.

ACCEPTANCE

And of course, the last stage is Acceptance, where you get to a sense of peace with whatever is going on around you.

During this stage, you stop fighting or trying to change the outcome, and accept the truth for what it is.

From a psychologist's standpoint—I'm hoping you see me as many things besides just that by now; a friend, daughter, equal, fellow believer, storyteller, radical survivor—if you are experiencing any emotion that is intensified following a loss, it may help to know that your reaction is quite natural.

It may be relieving to know that it's okay to cry. I can't stress this enough. It is okay to cry. It is okay to stop. It is okay to scream.

The goal is that even as you vent, your spirit continues to be cleansed and your strength renewed in the process. Remember you have to feel, to heal. Your laundry never gets washed while being stuffed away in your closet.

GROWTH THROUGH GRIEF

As mentioned, grief is not linear and can have many ups and downs, like a rollercoaster. There are also no rules when it comes to the timeline of grief. The tricky thing about loss is that there is no way to measure it. When something that meant the world to you vanishes in a matter of moments, life's sense of meaning and timeline are dismantled. As a result, some stretches of grief may be deeper and longer. Over time, the difficult periods should become less intense and shorter as time goes by.

But it takes time to work through a loss. After I lost my parents, special events would roll around—just because my world had stopped, doesn't mean that the world as a whole did. This gets confusing; big, happy moments and holidays don't feel the same anymore. Christmas and birthdays come and go and you're reminded that the lens through which you see, touch, feel, and experience your life just isn't the same anymore, and never will be.

Again, this isn't in a dooming way, but an honest one. And it's okay to be this honest and to note these changes! It's not complaining, it's not self-pity; it's being real and feeling—and you are wholly courageous each time you do this, because the only thing worse than the deep pain is numbness.

There's a hollowness in spending the holidays without the people you once loved, and it is okay to come to the realization that it takes time to adjust and process that information. You may have to remind yourself that it's for a season, and that it's going to get better. Again, this is about living in the present moment, sitting with your pain and being okay with it.

If you're someone who experiences anxiety, whether regularly, or just as a result of the onset of a new or stressful situation, then you know that fighting anxiety is what fuels it to become stronger.

The same goes with your pain. Instead of wrestling, fighting, ignoring or denying, let it come to you with acceptance. Over time, be open-minded and allow yourself to begin to enjoy again, because at some point, you are going to get back to that stage where you start enjoying life and living it to its fullest. Don't feel guilty when this day comes. Remember that the people you've lost adore you and want you to be happy. Finding joy is not an extension of forgetting that person or moving on, it's an extension of survival, gratitude, and honoring their memory by making the very most of the time you have here on Earth.

LIFE AUDIT AND NEGATIVITY CHECK DURING GRIEF

Understand that every resource that you need to be an overcomer exists on the inside. You have to declutter, but first you have to get to the stage where you feel ready to do so.

To declutter, you do a life audit and general negativity check. You take inventory of all of the relationships and situations in your life, whether that be work, where you live, the church you go to, how you spend your time, or what outside stressors you regularly expose yourself to. Oftentimes, many people inadvertently allow more pain in their lives by keeping energies around that are not helping them.

Do a vibe check. Sometimes people want to help but accidentally project their own pain, hang-ups, and challenges onto you. You don't have to allow this disruption of your peace to build up, explode, and bubble over. Instead, you can carefully zoom out and take a look at the situation from a birds-eye view—God's view.

Allow Him to lend you His eyes, wisdom, and discernment to show you the best way to navigate your ship out of this specific storm's reach.

You can still believe the best in people and maintain healthy boundaries at the same time. You're allowed to say no. Allow him to show you the best way.In some relationships, it may be through communication and setting boundaries, and with others, you may find that person unfortunately does not have a place in your life and doesn't have the ears to hear why. That's okay. You're allowed to create boundaries with actions instead of words.

God can show you the difference in these situations. When faced with loss and grief, not every person needs to be a part of the process with you. Choose those confidants who are consistent, resilient, and who are able to relate to your pain.

BECOMING A VICTOR INSTEAD OF A VICTIM

How do you overcome your grief? You tap into the pain. For the pain to be gutted, you have to actually get in. Think of it as an infection. For it to stop hurting and to heal you have to completely excavate it. You have to gash and squeeze the pus and infection out.

When you think of your grief, you have to get in there and begin the deep cleaning process. This may call for forgiveness. This might call for shifting, refocusing and realigning. You may find yourself looking in the rearview mirror. That's okay. You may see the errors that you've made. That's also okay.

In order for development, growth, and success to come to fruition, you have to come to terms with the fact that failing is part of it, and this does not mean you're a failure! It means you're growing and finding things that don't work.

This goes for absolutely everyone in the world—to succeed, you must first learn to fail.

What we all call "failure" is simply success turned inside-out. With great loss comes more room in our lives for greatness. Whatever it is that you have lost, whether it is finances, a marriage, a job, a promotion, a friendship, you're now stuck.

Remind yourself that you are your own resource. Remind yourself that everything you need to get out exists inside of you. Remind yourself that vulnerability is not weakness but actually strength.

You are what you eat. You hunger for what you feed on. Drink in positivity by the boatload. Listen or read self-help books and audiobooks. Hear the redemptive testimonies of others. Listen to podcasts. Sing along to upbeat songs. Read the Bible. Pray in love and expectation for the divine. Don't waste time wallowing in self-pity and the "woe is me" mentality. Sometimes when we are feeling pain, we soothe that pain by listening to sad songs and poetry, but you must do the complete opposite to be an overcomer.

Move from the space of being a survivor to being a thriver—from a victim to a victor. This is not to be misconstrued as negating or forgetting all that you have experienced as far as loss, but rather how you use a particular loss to drive you to productively seeking the best for yourself.

BOTTOM LINE: KEEP GAINING MOMENTUM

One of the most important things I would say is that even as you surrender or slow down, don't stop. Don't stop trying and don't stop moving because whenever you stop, it is more difficult to get back into the rhythm of actually moving.

Nothing under the sun is new; everything is basically a regurgitation. It has been done before, it has been seen before, it has been felt before—perhaps not by you as an individual, but by someone else. That does not discredit our experience or make it unimportant; however, it does mean that there are persons who have experienced similar and have overcome to emerge on the other side.

You are going to thrive, motivate, and inspire.

It's written in you.

CHAPTER FOUR

LIFE'S SEASONS

"There is a time for everything under Heaven."

I grew up hearing this statement, which basically meant that time and seasons change. Nothing lasts forever and we are expected to have highs and lows, the good and the ugly.

The reality is that we would all prefer to only experience the high, mountain-top experiences. But truth be told, it is in the valley moments that we are strengthened, developed, and refined.

Being born in the Caribbean, I was never privy to experience the meteorological change of seasons. We were subjected to only sun, rain, day, or night with the occasional hurricane.

I became quite fond of the change in seasons I came to know in North America and the U.K.: winter, spring, summer, and fall. I would want to believe that the people living in these locations may have learned to live in anticipation of the beginning and end of each of these seasons for different reasons. Allow me to use the seasons to describe the intricate changes of life.

SEASON #1: WINTER – REFLECTING

Winter always makes me think of dark winter storms. As I reminisce while writing this, winter still makes me think about the fatal moment my mother took her final breath seven years ago. As you can imagine, life undoubtedly changed forever for me at that point.

The winter season ironically falls at the start of the year, when most will be in a highly anticipatory mood of all the new experiences to come that year. Paradoxically, the thought of winter also signals dormancy. It is as if all of nature is dead and lifeless, and the world is merely resting.

During the winter season, the general mood suggests a quiet contemplation, a time to slow down and conserve one's energy. A time to bundle up and stay indoors, to shelter from the cold.

Similar to winter, unexpected loss can signal that it's time to stop in our tracks and reassess, reevaluate and reflect. This loss could come in the form of the passing of a loved one, threat or diagnosis of a disease, impending economic doom, or unwarranted betrayal.

Perhaps that's why we often see so many resolutions to begin the year. If you're anything like me, these resolutions all too often become an abstract aspiration. A glimmer of spring sparkles in the distance and the perspectives, resolve, and emotional tenacity experienced during our winter season often fade away.

SEASON #2: SPRING – BREATHING AND BELIEVING

Here comes spring, which symbolically represents bouncing back from the harshness of winter.

We feel the energy of something new—beginnings, progress, abundance. We get the notion that new things are ready to blossom: birth, life, opportunity, or even business.

Springtime gives us hope that our lives can be transformed and new possibilities can emerge. This is the time that I feel most like I can exhale and begin believing again. Just as I feel at peace when I see a newborn baby or flowers blossoming in nature, spring tells me that my future can be bright if I continue to believe in all good things such as love, joy, kindness, beauty, justice, and gratitude. Spring is a positive outlook in a negative world; spring is a stranger smiling at you.

Just like with spring cleaning, spring means out with the old and in with the new.

SEASON #3: SUMMER - GOAL-SETTING AND GO-GETTING

Summer brings with it a youthful exuberance. This is a time when you kickstart every project, dream, or plan you've ever imagined.

There is an energy in the air during summer that emerges as you work towards achieving goal after goal. It calls for tenacity and relentless drive that says no obstacle is too big, that nothing can deter you, derail you, or slow you down.

In the summertime, the vision board becomes your focus point, like the shining sun that seems to always be hanging out in the sky, ready to warm your skin and set your dreams aflame. The clarity of thought and direction is unmatched and allows you to seek out the right alignments.

The appreciation of your words and values becomes paramount because now there is absolutely no willingness to settle for less than your worth. You're at a point where you will be willing to sit at the table alone if that is what it took for you not to compromise your brand.

In the summertime, the CEO emerges unapologetically. And that CEO is you, safeguarding your brand at all costs.

SEASON #4: AUTUMN - HARVESTING

Here comes fall, or autumn. This is maturity season— the time to harvest the results of your summer season. The time to reap the fruits of your labor.

Though harvesting is not all about receiving with ease, autumn is super fulfilling. From a spiritual standpoint, harvesting during fall represents a time to acknowledge growth and expansion as a natural evolution of being.

It was in my autumn season that I put my pain in perspective and looked at my journey from being a victim of divorce, from being made an adult orphan, from the countless betrayals, to becoming not only a survivor of these hardships but a thriver. In my autumn season, I learned to transform these experiences into something productive that can help others. I saw the realization of a support group for women who had experienced a broken romantic relationship. I founded a cancer support foundation to assist patients and families of patients diagnosed with cancer here in St. Vincent. We are often not only the emotional and spiritual support for survivors, but also the financial support to assist them in receiving treatment abroad.

It was in my autumn season I can say I became one with myself. My faith was tested, strengthened and restored.

YOUR FULL EVOLUTION OF SELF AFTER GOING THROUGH EACH SEASON

I am now on a path of self-actualization where I enjoy authenticity, honesty, living at my best, and being the best version of myself each day. I have learned that having a good heart and the right motives are the ingredients needed to turn your life around. For me, those two things are the bridge to the formula, as love cancels and covers a multitude of sins.

If you can't change the people around you geographically, then you can change the people around you mentally, psychologically, and emotionally. Use your good to be the change you want to see in the world around you.

I believe that a breakdown should never be an option. If we realize that it is okay to stop, feel the emotions as you experience them, but not wallow in them, then getting to a point of combustion shouldn't need to happen. Rather, keep going, keep pressing, and keep bouncing back.

The song "I Hope You Dance" by LeeAnn Womack, sums it up, and has become an anthem of sorts for me personally:

I hope you never lose your sense of wonder,

You get your fill to eat but always keep the hunger,

May you never take one single breath for granted,

God forbid love ever leave you empty-handed,

I hope you still feel small when you stand beside the ocean,

Whenever one door closes I hope one more opens,

Promise me that you'll give faith a fighting chance,

And when you get the choice to sit it out or dance,

I hope you dance,

I hope you never fear those mountains in the distance,

Never settle for the path of least resistance,

Living might mean taking chances, but they were taken,

Loving might be a mistake but it's worth making,

Don't let some hell bent heart leave you bitter,

When you come close to selling out reconsider,

Give the Heavens above more than just a passing glance,

And when you get the choice to sit it out or dance,

I hope you dance.

I say to myself every day, keep dancing, Jozelle. As the rhythm of life plays on, keep dancing.

It is paramount that at the end of each stage and season that each individual gets to the place of understanding self-governance. We're no longer projecting from a place of hurt and pain, but rather regulating those negative emotions and setting a new path in place. We've become goal-crushers. We set daily goals and we remain deliberate and purposeful in achieving them.

YOUR FULL DESTRUCTION OF SELF IF YOU OVERSTAY YOUR WELCOME IN ONE STAGE

Goal-setting is a means of remaining focused, providing direction to the next level, helping to navigate the season, all unto knowing when it is time to transition.

When you've outgrown a season and you refuse to move, or if you are afraid to let go or face the unknown, it will undoubtedly lead to frustration and unnecessary conflict, rendering the energy in that space counterproductive. Once the goals have been achieved and the learning curve reached, the growth becomes stagnated. To become a butterfly, you must break out of the cocoon. Stagnation leads to death. Death fuels bacteria and infection. When blood flow stops, deterioration begins. Simply put, if you are not growing, you are ultimately dying.

I remember when my marriage was coming to an end; my husband was resolute in his destructive and hurtful actions towards me. He was blatant in his disrespect; he didn't care anymore to be discreet, hide or pretend, or to hold onto or believe in any glimmer of hope that our marriage could work. Living in that space with him became unbearable; his actions became mean and callous. He was no longer my husband, regardless of what a legal marriage license said, but instead a shell of the man I once knew and had fallen in love with. He now belonged to someone else.

In trying to hold on to that dead thing, I lost myself and became someone I no longer recognized. I found myself lost, in places I shouldn't be, trying to get a glimpse of him being unfaithful. I was probably just trying to prove to myself yet again that it was real. Remember the denial stage we talked about earlier in this book?

I knew it well. I was checking phones, emails, and so on. I was driving myself crazy, or rather, allowing him to drive me crazy. I was being publicly disrespected by him, laughed at by others. He was openly and unabashedly mocking the love and trust between us that had taken years to build.

Who the heck was I at that point really? I certainly didn't recognize myself. My confidence was shot; I was angry, bitter, and lost.

This is what typically happens when you stay too long in a season that has already changed. Opportunities are missed, joy and peace are stripped away, the restlessness becomes unnerving, and your identity disappears.

SIGNS IT'S TIME TO EVOLVE TO THE NEXT SEASON AND STAGE

How do you identify when you've outlived a space? I would suggest looking for these signs:

SIGN #1:

You have a sense of restlessness.

HOW THIS MANIFESTS:

This is usually one of the first signs you will experience when God starts to prepare you for a transition. You begin to feel ready for a change, even if you're not sure what kind of change. You start to feel restless about where you're at. Many times, your passion for what you're doing will also begin to fade.

For example, perhaps you have been on fire while serving in a particular ministry or job for years. Then all of a sudden that fire goes out and you don't have the same desire to serve in that capacity like you once did. That may be a sign that God is getting you ready to move you to the next space, the next place of service. It is important to note that this sense of restlessness isn't the same as being burned out. It's not brought on by overwork, stress, or exhaustion. Rather, usually nothing has changed externally, but there has been an internal shift in your thoughts and feelings about where you're at.

WHAT TO DO NEXT:

When you sense that change, start praying and ask God why you're feeling that way. It could be just a passing phase, or it could be God preparing to move you into another season.

SIGN #2:

Things aren't working out and doors are closing.

HOW THIS MANIFESTS:

This one used to frustrate me, but I've learned that closed doors are God's hands of protection and preparation. A great example of this in scripture is in Acts 16:6-10 when Paul and his companions were prevented by the Holy Spirit from ministering in certain places. Doors within the ministry kept closing and yet Paul kept trying new doors.

Eventually, Paul received a vision about a man from Macedonia asking for help and Paul discerned that God was telling him to go there.

WHAT TO DO NEXT:

Just like Paul, if doors keep closing for you and nothing you're trying is working out when it comes to new ventures, it may be that God is the one keeping you from those things.

This isn't a punishment, but rather that He has something better in store for you.

When doors start closing and you're running out of ideas and options, start praying and asking God to lead you to an open door. Also, ask Him if there is anything He needs to do within you to prepare for that open door.

During every transitional season, there is almost always some type of preparation or pruning that the Lord will want to do in our lives, so we have to be open to that.

SIGN #3:

Unexpected opportunities pop up and doors will begin to open.

HOW THIS MANIFESTS:

When things start happening out of the blue, like new opportunities that you weren't looking for arising, or new relationships or connections that you didn't see coming happening, it's usually a sign that God is giving you the first few steps towards your new season.

It can feel confusing at first, but it quickly becomes exciting as you start seeing new possibilities. Esther, Joseph, and David are just a few examples in the Bible of people who experience comparable circumstances outside of their control. Each time God was the one moving and working behind the scenes to bring them to a place of greater service for His glory.

WHAT TO DO NEXT:

If you see an unexpected door opening on the horizon, don't run from it, prayerfully approach it.

SIGN #4:

You notice a recurring theme or burden related to a new calling.

HOW THIS MANIFESTS:

If certain topics keep appearing, God may be sending signals that seem to be related to your new season. For example, if you suddenly keep hearing about a certain location or a particular job, God may be trying to turn your attention towards a new direction.

Sometimes we also begin to have a burden for something we didn't have before. For instance, you might have a burden for the elderly or the children, or you have a burden to see young people living purposeful lives, or something comparable. This means that God is now giving you new insight.

WHAT TO DO NEXT:

Approach this God-given insight carefully, and prayerfully begin asking the Lord for direction. The key to navigating a season change is to stay surrendered in prayer.

At times you don't have any clarity at all about what God is doing in your life. I certainly have gone through many different points of my life without clarity, where I have to depend solely on God to open my eyes and reveal what He is doing in that time and season.

But most of the time, we can sense and notice a change is coming. God created us with that intuition and instinct for a purpose.

If you are in a season where you know God is leading you to some sort of change, but you have no idea what it looks like, stay connected to Him. Stay connected in prayer and fasting and reading His word. The puzzle will begin to fall into place; finally you will start seeing the pieces come together. It's easy to become bored or frustrated with where you are currently at.

It can be even easier to try to rush a season change, but we can't allow ourselves to get distracted by what is going on around us. We can't keep looking at what other people are doing; we can't compare their progression and success to ours, because comparison is a thief of joy. I always say to stay in your own lane and keep your eyes on the road and where you yourself are heading. Looking to the side could cause you to crash. Where others are headed isn't your business anyway!

We have to always remember that everyone's journey is different. We have to stay surrendered to God for His timing and for His way. His timing is perfect.

Yes, the waiting is hard, but I have learned to stay focused, obedient, and to seek to glorify God in every single thing I do. It is SO not about me. Even as I wait for my season to change, I wait in Him, and in His perfect peace. God will not only bring out His plans for our lives, but He will also conform, establish, and bless them above anything we could ever imagine or create. That is a promise that He has made to us: "Now to him who is able to do immeasurably more than all we ask or imagine, according to his power that is at work within us, to him be glory in thee." (Ephesians 3:20)

Additionally, Mark 16:6-7 says,

You are looking for Jesus the Nazarene who was crucified.

He has risen, He is not here.

See the place where they laid him?

But go, tell His disciples, and, Peter, He is going ahead of you into Galilee and there you will see Him just as He told you.

When Mary Magdalene and two other women went to Jesus' tomb after his death, an Angel said to them,

'He is not here, He is risen. He has gone ahead of you into Galilee then you will see him.'

Notice the Angel said He is not here, He is there. The Angel was saying, in effect, I know you're hurting, but don't stay here, something better is waiting for you there. In other words, here is a disappointment, the bad medical reports, the dream that didn't work out. If you stay here, you will be discouraged. You have to go there.

Sometimes the reason God doesn't comfort us in the "here," or in the disappointment, is because He doesn't want us to stay where we are. It's not the place He has designed for us, and our growing pains are evidence of that.

"There" is where God is waiting for you. "There" is where the blessing is.

The disappointment is simply a season. God has already gone ahead and lined up the next level. Move forward into your day! Move forward into your new season. Grab hold of His hand. Follow His lead unto obedience which yields abundance.

CHAPTER FIVE

MOSES HAD A STAFF - WHAT INNATE, UNIQUE GIFTS ARE IN YOUR HANDS TO EQUIP YOU?

The greatest resource we have to bounce back from life's challenges is on the inside of us. It speaks not only to our innate grit, but also to the purpose for which we were created and the skillset we possess.

The sad reality is that we often overlook the potential within us, too busy seeking out external remedies to notice and listen to the treasures that are inside.

What I believe God wants to remind us is to use what is in our hearts and hands. I reference a story of Moses leading the Israelites out of captivity: Moses and the Israelites are in a difficult place. As many of us experience from time to time, their backs were against the wall. Backed into a corner, with their enemy right on top of them, close enough to bite them, and the deep Red Sea before them.

God ordered Moses to stretch out his staff over the Red Sea and, as a result, the sea parted. This allowed the Israelites to escape across the sea and away from Egypt unharmed. Meanwhile, the Pharaoh and his army followed them by charging into the sea, but Moses waved his staff and the sea returned to its normal height, swallowing up the entire army of the Pharaoh.

I can certainly identify with this narrative of being in situations where it felt that other people were all out to kill me emotionally, and feeling hopeless in terms of my options to move forward. These were the moments God spoke to me, as he did to Moses about using what is in his hand. The question I always ask myself is, "What are you holding in your hand, Jozelle?"

So often we look beyond ourselves for help, fantasizing about the knight in shining armor who sweeps in and saves the day. But we never see ourselves being equipped with what it takes in that moment to change our own situations. I remember hearing a quote that read, "You never know how strong you are, until being strong is the only option you had left."

I firmly believe that in my case, because of the way that my gift or purpose in life has always been to touch the lives of others in an impactful way. I always felt that psychology found me as opposed to having been chosen by me. As God would have it, my natural knack for helping people has always been my go-to coping mechanism.

I firmly believe that nothing just "happens" when your life is ordered by God. There are coincidences, and there are constructions—moments constructed by God. He allows things to unfold in a particular way to teach us, to mold us, and create within us the virtues needed to represent Him in the cold dark world.

So, with that understanding, I believe that our experiences were not about us. It is for us to endure it, yes, but we are to use our testimonies to assist other people through their difficult experiences.

YOUR TESTIMONY

One of the things in your hands is your testimony. The scripture reminds us in Revelation 12:11, "And they overcame him by the blood of the lamb and by the word of their testimony."

REASONS TO SHARE YOUR TESTIMONY:

REASON #1: Your story is unique, even if you don't think so.

It is such a blessing to remember that moment when we discover Jesus to be our Lord and Savior. The moment, special and unique only to yours and His relationship, where you repent of ALL of your wrong-doings and then BELIEVE.

This is a miraculous moment; a weight lifted and a life cleansed and renewed. A barrier of sin broken, and a binding bridge of unconditional love and grace replacing it. In fact, it could undoubtedly be one of the most memorable days of a believer's life.

It is so very important that we release our stories and allow the enemy to know that we are victorious. Whether you are addicted to drugs, alcohol, or technology, the Savior held you through your breakthrough. You found Jesus, who gives you constant hope and unshakable strength to continue onward in the midst of a disheveled world.

Did you get into trouble with the law and then realize how much you would have messed up your life? Did you miss out on some seemingly wonderful opportunities? But did you then realize that things work out okay because God loves you and He has promised never to leave you nor forsake you?

Above all our messed up carnal or self-serving tendencies, He has promised that whatever the enemy meant for bad, He can turn around for the good.

At some point, we all realize that life wasn't working out so well when we were running things in our own way, calling the shots, and pulling the strings. We have to get to the point of understanding that we need help. People can usually run their lives just fine when things are going well, but when problems strike, we always need another perspective.

Our testimony may have been extreme in some cases, even radical, or it might have been a calm profession of our belief and our truth. Either way, both types of testimonies depict God's love and mercy, and neither is worth more than the other, because all of us have sinned and come short of the Glory of God.

REASON #2: God's Word tells us to share our hope as a believer.

1 Peter 3:15-16 reads,

But in your heart revere Christ as Lord.

Always be prepared to give an answer to everyone who asks you to give the reason for the hope that you have,

but do this with gentleness and respect,

keeping a clear conscience so that those who speak maliciously against your good behavior in Christ may be ashamed of their slander.

This verse reminds me to worship Christ as Lord of my life. If someone asks about your hope as a believer, always be ready to explain gently and share your story.

REASON #3: People love stories.

That's one thing I've learned about people, regardless of religion or belief system. Our testimony is a story, and we all have stories. People enjoy going to the movies, immersing themselves in books, and listening to stories that they can imagine in their minds.

When we share our stories, it also helps to connect people to our lives and in turn, better connect with their own lives and situations. Stories show what happens behind the curtains; they humanize the images we sometimes put out into the world, the pretenses. Stories bring resemblances between characters, both in real life and in fiction, to what we have endured, by creating an opening for them to get over to the other side and into another's life.

Testimonies help to remove fears and give courage. In speaking about what God has done in our lives, we are also remembering all of God's goodness. When we recount the blessings of Jesus and all He has done for us in the past, it gives us all more faith and courage for our present situation, and hope about our futures.

When the Israelites remembered all that God had done for them in the past, such as bringing them out of Egypt, they had the courage to continue onward into the Promised Land. When Jesus's disciples thought back on all He had taught them, they were able to spread Jesus's life story to others and share it as a great commission.

REASON #4: Any story that shows how good God is or how He has worked miraculously is worth sharing.

A redemptive story can become far more than just a story. It has the power to become a resource. I am proof of the power of God for those who need something to hang onto.

Testimonies show that there isn't any situation that is too big, that there is evidence we have and can reference to truly know and remember that Christ can fix and change any situation. Nothing is too late or too far gone for Him.

Even this book is a testimony of God and a gift and blessing where anyone who reads it can feel connected to me because of the transparency it not only represents but also holds inside. I've spelled out all that I've gone through in my life, from my divorce to the death of my parents.

YOUR UNIQUE GIFTS AND TALENTS

Moses had his staff. You have your testimony, and another thing in your hands equipping you is your skillset.

For me personally, that was becoming a psychologist. As a child, my interest was to become a medical doctor, but my calling took another direction. I was drawn to speaking with people about their life's challenges and working towards helping them lead more fulfilling lives. So I worked hard, put in long hours to refine my craft, and built a brand that was accountable and reliable as a therapist. It took me just about 13 years to move from a bachelor's degree to a Ph.D. qualification in psychology.

I journeyed from St. Vincent to Jamaica, to Grenada, and to the U.K. It took a lot of adjusting to the various cultures, remaining focused, and clinging onto the constant faith I knew in my heart while being away from my support system.

The Ph.D. was especially significant for me, as it has always been a dream of mine and also of my mom's. The thought, heart, and intention behind this large goal was that I would dedicate this degree to my mom. I wanted to make both of my parents proud. The sad thing is that the moment when I accomplished the highest achievement of my academic career, I felt very alone. It was a time when my marriage was literally on the rocks and my mom had already been diagnosed with cancer.

I remember calling her when I completed my dissertation defense, and I heard the pain in her voice as she tried to muster up the strength to be excited for me. She said, "God bless you, baby, thank God for you."

When I got off the phone, I felt the deepest sadness. All the euphoric anticipation disappeared, and my joy was replaced by fear. I was so scared as I was losing my mom that I didn't celebrate. I didn't have a chance to feel happy and truly appreciate the end result of all my hard work. I cried and cried, feeling truly robbed of the opportunity.

After the test, I started feeling bitter and upset with my ex-husband, as he had abandoned me in the process. I felt abandoned by my family as well.

I've learned that sometimes you just have to encourage yourself. Sing your own praises, because you may never have a cheering squad around when you need it most.

IS IT POSSIBLE TO FEEL HAPPY AND SAD AT SAME TIME?

Saudade means being nostalgic, happy, and sad all at the same time. This is the clearest demonstration of mixed emotions—the question of whether it is possible to feel happy and sad at the same time. A psychology professor at the University of Tennessee, Knoxville responded that the emotional landscape is laid out in such a way that we are feeling one way or the other, or neither.

There are times, however, when we may feel bored. Scenarios that often trigger our happy and sad state include bittersweet events like graduations, moving, or migrating to another country. These are situations that warrant mixed feelings, being sad about one thing but happy or excited about another. Endings that are also beginnings tend to have an emotional limbo type of feeling when you are sad, happy, and a mixed bag of emotions at the same time.

Our minds then will have to learn to adapt and process the information differently. What helps me is Proverbs 18:16: "A man's gift opens doors for him, and brings him before great men." In short, we are to use what is in our hands to change our lives. God has carefully and intentionally placed specific and unique gifts and talents in each and every one of us. This gives us a purpose no one else can fill. During those times when we may get so low that we feel like we have nothing else to live for, this is what we should remember.

Our gift will carve room for us into the world and bring before us great opportunities. It is a gift that we have that will enable us to fulfill our vision. It will make a way for us in our darkest situation, and it will help us to feel a sense of real fulfillment, purpose, and contentment in our work.

It is interesting to know that the Bible does not say that a man's education makes room for him, but rather his gift. His gift speaks of his purpose. Somehow, we have swallowed the idea that education is the key to success. Our families and societies have reinforced the idea towards both.

We'll have to change our perspective if we are to truly be successful. Education is not the key to success. I'm not saying that we should not seek to educate ourselves, but in terms of securing financial security and freedom, it is not going to be obtained during our 9 to 5 jobs. It is not what education would afford us, but it is what our purpose and our gifting would afford us!

If you are intelligent but are not exercising your gift, you are probably going to be poor. If you are educated but have never developed your talent, you're likely to be depressed, frustrated, and tired. You're always going to be exhausted and frustrated by the thought of going to work on Monday morning. You'll live for the weekends, the breathers in between, instead of maintaining a full life no matter what the day is. Education can afford you a job, and that provides some needed security, but it is often not what takes you to the next level of success.

The second part of the aforementioned Proverb focuses on our giftings bringing us before great men. You don't realize that the gift you have is what is going to propel you or pull you back so far that your trajectory, whenever you are released, is going to take you into significantly elevated spaces. You will sit around princes and princesses, kings and queens, presidents and prime ministers, because of the elevation that your gift is going to afford you.

I believe, even as I write this book, that it is my gift that is going to allow me to extend to higher heights; to bring me to inspirational, motivational, and like-minded speakers who are also thriving in their own skillsets.

It is important, therefore, that each and every individual take the time to figure out what their God-given gift and purpose is. We discover this by introspection, by going over our values, beliefs, and connecting with our inner voice. We discover our gifts and purposes by tapping into our conscience, the still, small voice that speaks to and directs us. As we are directed, we need to be obedient.

Alexander Graham Bell believed that sound could be converted into electrical impulses and transmitted by wire. A lot of people thought he was crazy, but this "crazy" person, who had that grand idea, stuck it out, and as a result, we are now gifted with the telephone and different versions of it.

Sometimes when you are gifted, it means you have to walk alone and listen to that voice no matter what. It means that your position in life will not allow you to have cheerleaders around you. Many people may not have the vision or the insight, but you have to stay your ground, because He who has begun a work in you wants to bring that planted seed to full fruition.

I will always believe and stand by that where there's a will, there is a way. We have to use what is in our hands to pivot, to get crafty, to think out of the box to solve problems with innovation, instead of fixating on the problem itself. We have to understand that sometimes in using what is in our hands, we must be stretched in new ways, at times pulled back in the way that may seem like a failure. However, just like a slingshot, when we are released, we will propel forward.

It will be supernatural and an experience like none other.

CHAPTER SIX

WAITING FOR GOD OR WAITING IN GOD?

Eventually, we all have to make a choice whether to continue swimming upstream, going against the current and waves, or relaxing and allowing the waves from the songs of life to work on our behalf.

I refer to the scripture in Genesis 50:20, "As for you, you mean it against me, but God meant it for good. To bring it about, that many people should be kept alive as they are today."

I also refer to Romans 8:28, "As we know that for those who love God all things work together for good, for those who are called to call into His purpose."

The events of life can be daunting, yes? They can leave us with so many questions. We can spend a lifetime sobbing about the unfairness of life's situations, we can spend a lifetime asking the Lord why. This is where I was for a long time in the past, but I quickly came to the realization that

God allows the hardest tests to come to His best soldiers. I remember Job and that question, "What can the enemy do to us without God's permission, really?"

What he allows must be to accomplish a greater good. That's how I came to the point where I saw my adversity as a means by which God can work in me and through me. It was through my adversities that he set me on a path to accomplish His will. Psalms 119:71 points out, "It is good for me that I've been afflicted, that I might learn thy statutes."

The moment I truly understood that nothing happens by chance, that everything must work for the Glory and Honor of God, was also the moment I appreciated that giving our lives to the Lord should make us realize that we exist to do His Will in all that we do. As such, we are to surrender to His precepts.

Surrendering and giving everything means that the body that we live and exist in is merely a temporary loan. It is merely an earthly vehicle for our spirit, soul, and mind to connect with God so that we can do what He would want to be done here on Earth as His vessels.

God being in complete control has new meaning for us. He does not have SOME control but rather ALL control. How much peace is there in knowing that?!

In the passing of my parents, He was in control. Through my divorce, He was in control. He was also in control when I learned I was unable to medically conceive a child. He was in control when I made it through my Ph.D. amidst all the personal challenges. God takes care of His own. Period. Let us never lose sight of that.

So, to relax in the Lord's control basically means that "Whatever the future holds, my Faith will see me through," to use a line from my national anthem.

Not my actions, crying, or merely praying, but rather my complete and total faith in the One who holds the future will see me through my challenges.

I trust the transitioning of seasons in my life, never within my own timing or on my clock, but always at the time divinely orchestrated by God.

This was a big one for me: life is not by my own time.

I'm one of the most impatient people that lives today. And literally, I had to get to the place of understanding that God's timing is perfect. So I learned what it means to not wait on God but rather to wait in God. There is a big difference between "waiting for" and "waiting in." "Waiting for" means using your own timing as a reference, whereas "waiting in" means resting and believing in His own timing.

Get busy with the things of God, with being productive, impactful, purposeful, and being Kingdom-minded. Being Kingdom-minded gets the focus off yourself and tuned into higher frequencies only God has. Being Kingdom-minded takes away a lot of the frustration of sitting and waiting, looking at the clock, because now you aren't focusing on what you see physically on Earth. You are engaged with the Divine, and time moves differently.

Going with the waves taught me about the need to be open-minded and embrace new things. But also, most importantly, it suggests the importance of being flexible in the face of trauma.

FLEXIBILITY IN THE FACE OF TRAUMA

The question then, is what does flexibility really mean? The word flexibility technically means the ability to bend without breaking. However, people often use it to describe the ability to adjust to the changes in your life without creating stress or drama. Being flexible in life means that you can change your plans and adapt to new situations easily. Flexibility is important in your everyday life for a variety of reasons.

FLEXIBILITY BENEFIT #1: Being flexible can help you avoid being overwhelmed or stifled by change.

You will also have an increased ability to direct your

development and personal life rather than being a passive participant.

Some of the other benefits of flexibility include having a sense of adaptability to change. While I know that the only constant in life is change, I understand fully why we are all afraid of change at some point.

We fear change because it means that the outcomes are unknown. Our brains are designed to find peace in knowing, and, when we don't know what will happen, we make up scenarios and in turn create worry. Humans, additionally, find it hard to move on when something known comes to an end.

The fear of failure also comes into play to create a fear of change. If we don't know how something will turn out, we may not try because the outcome could be bad. Flexibility also helps with managing the unexpected. In many cases, an unexpected event can require adaptability. For example, you may need to pick your child up from school early because they are sick. In this case, you need to calmly respond to the situation. For instance, you may be able to arrange to work from home, so you can address all of your responsibilities at the same time.

Flexibility allows for life satisfaction. It reduces stress and exposes you to new experiences, which, if you ask me, is one of the biggest parts of leading a happy and successful life.

FLEXIBILITY BENEFIT #2: Flexibility fosters vulnerability.

This is without a doubt one of the biggest fears of every individual. Vulnerability is a quality or state of being exposed to the possibility of being attacked or harmed, either physically or emotionally. We equate vulnerability with weakness. An honest revelation of our feelings puts us in a dangerous place of letting down our defenses.

I remember being so scared, to the point of literally shaking, to speak about my own divorce. I knew I'd be subjected to judgment, assumptions, and the dreaded public opinion, especially in the small country of St. Vincent and the Grenadines. But I got to a point where I could no longer keep it bottled up on the inside, and vulnerability became my healing space, my place to break free and let go.

Vulnerability became where I connected with how I felt. Vulnerability is the foundation of healing.

I was now in a position to start moving again, so I had to ask for what I needed.

When we are hurting, it's easy to dismiss our pain and try to protect ourselves and the people around us by closing off. However, achieving close connections means being willing to speak up when you're in need. I had to get to the place where I actually asked people for help by communicating exactly what I needed at that moment.

Admitting that we need someone to lean on, that we

are struggling or need help, allows our loved ones to feel for us and respond in ways that help bring us closer. Being vulnerable helps me expose my feelings while forming new connections with other people who feel the same way and are going through similar things. It took practice but by following that process, I created a supportive network for myself and others.

When we are going through hard seasons, we expect people to know how to respond or what to do at any given time. This sets everyone up for failure. Instead, we must be willing to put down our defenses, change our body language and attitude, and set everything else aside, even our own pride, and just simply ask specifically for what we want at the time that we want it.

Do not be afraid of being judged as being bossy or pushy. See yourself through a beautiful light by commending your own courage to be assertive, authentic, and open. Be honest about your point of view and check in with your real self. It doesn't mean being insensitive or unnecessarily hurtful, but it does mean that you allow for an authentic exchange and interaction.

FLEXIBILITY BENEFIT #3: Flexibility and vulnerability alike require you to slow down and listen to God and your inner voice.

Being vulnerable taught me to slow down, stop myself from doing too much, and just simply be there in the moment.

Yes, the state of vulnerability is incredibly uncomfortable because all of the negative emotions were there. The pain, the hurt, the memories—the gang was all there.

But I had to allow that cloud to pass, and then the sun began shining in.

FLEXIBILITY BENEFIT #4: You allow yourself to stop and assess the moment to check if the current time is best spent covering your own needs or the needs of others. This promotes balance.

You can't pour out from an empty vessel, and when you try to, you can burn out.

I remember once being told that I self-sacrifice too much. It went all the way back to my childhood and feeling as if my responsibility was to take care of others and to make others happy, especially my mom. I lived in her shadow to the extent that everything I did was about her, what she wanted,

Dr. Jozelle M. Miller | 91

and what she needed. In some instances, I allowed my own needs, wants, and desires to fade away in the background.

But I'm at a point now where self-care is totally mandatory in my life. I realize and understand fully now that it is my God-given constitution to take care of myself first.

A great example of this is on flights, in the case of an emergency, you are instructed to put on your mask first. There is nothing selfish in prioritizing yourself, but it can be very difficult for people who have spent so long thinking differently. It requires a whole unpacking and deconstructing of a mindset that has become a distinct part of yourself and identity for so long.

Nonetheless, I had to learn that taking care of myself put me in a better position to take care of others. We have to invest in ourselves! Even writing this book is part of my own self-care process, and actually choosing my own dreams and my desires.

HOW TO SELF-CARE

Some of my go-to self-care habits include making sure I live a healthy life by eating healthy foods, getting enough sleep as often as I can, and exercising regularly.

I don't take drugs, or drink alcohol. I manage stress and do my medical check-ups.

I filter a lot of toxicity out of my life by taking away anything that I feel robs me or lessens who I am as my best self.

I have become more than okay with telling others no. I have also become more than okay with others telling me no. I have become even more okay with God telling me no. I know that sometimes "no" is a true no, meaning never, and other times, "no" simply means "not now," rather than "not ever."

I understand fully what it is to say goodbye, and as a matter of fact, I think part of my self-care that God has given me is the gift of goodbye. I have grown to be able to easily say goodbye to certain things and people with an expiration date, realizing that letting go is healthy. If we never let go, we will always be inhaling, holding our breath. There is a reason why we exhale, there is a reason why we sleep at night, and there is a reason for pauses; letting go is pivotal.

Before these realizations, though, we tend to try to tighten our grasp, don't we? We tend to try to hold onto situations, people, and seasons with a sense of deep ownership, as if these things ever were ours to begin with. This goes back to being stagnant and wanting to stay in a season or allowing ourselves to linger despite an eviction notice. It can be out of a sense of false obligation, but now we can learn to be fully obligated to taking care of ourselves.

We can focus on practicing good hygiene, which is important for social, medical, and psychological reasons. We can focus on trying to reduce the risk of illness, working toward being more preventative than curative.

We can allow ourselves to identify deeply with friends and family to help build our senses of belonging. We are no longer doomed to shame or self-isolation, but rather can seek efforts to integrate love into our lives as much as we possibly can. To be a part of the process of life with one another, and to engage others meaningfully.

We can try to do something we enjoy every day, whether it's dancing, watching a favorite movie, reading, or eating something that we really like. We can free ourselves to simply do something specific for our own personal enjoyment. We can find ways to relax like go to the spa, have a massage, or sit on the beach and listen to the waves to refresh and rejuvenate ourselves. Once it's safe to do so again, we can travel. These things have all been part of my self-care routine, and I hope that they can become part of yours, too!

Every person should design a self-care plan. For your plan, pay close attention to the things that are stressors in your life. Ask yourself these critical questions:

- **Why does this situation or person bother me?**

- **What can I shift to start feeling better about this situation or person?**

- Is a rational, kind, peaceful, and intentional removal of that situation or person needed?

- Are there things inside myself that need to shift?

- Am I taking an honest inventory of my own self?

- What are my current coping strategies?

- Are they working well for me?

- Am I having a lot of negative thoughts?

- What are those negative thoughts?

- How can I reframe those negative thoughts?

- What is my plan for reframing them at the moment of rapid occurrence?

There is a lesson to be learned no matter what the situation is.

There is no growth without change, even if it's a small change.

When lessons are truly learned, and actually stick, it makes it difficult for mistakes to be repeated.

I'm a firm believer that the incidents and previous traumas—great or small—that we do not heal from control, dictate, and take away from our lives.

For instance, I have seen so many of my friends end up in the same type of relationship—exactly the same character and dynamic, just with a different person. This is because we may think we have healed because we have changed the aesthetic, or the outside of a thing, but healing takes a lot longer on the inside.

When I think of patients who receive surgery, it's quite interesting how the healing time for our internal and external bodies differ completely. While someone can appear healed from the outside, their inner tissues take much longer.

The very same thing applies to life: if we do not take the time to heal on the inside, we run the risk of getting involved in the same exact scenarios over and over again—the same relationship, different person. The same arguments that we keep having, just with different people and in different situations.

The aim, really and truly in life, is to understand where you're at. Use the resources that exist inside of you, and keep it moving, even when one chapter ends. Even if it did not end the way you anticipated it to end, you must continue to take the pen to paper and continue the narrative.

We begin to scribe and our Author and Creator is faithful in ensuring the script of the new chapter is better, so long as we've learned our lessons. At this stage, we have been pruned and prodded, never perfect but always purposeful, and we reach the point of self-actualization.

We're no longer bound or imprisoned by external forces, and we know what it is to exist in a world where a lot of things are happening outside of and around you. We're free from our inner prison where we cannot see outside of our hardships, but this doesn't mean the work is over. We have to continue the good fight and choose our personal and internal spaces of peace.

Reaching self-actualization doesn't mean you'll never fall down again, but rather that when you do, you don't stay down, you get back up. You understand that it is not about you, and it's not about us. We lived the story, but we survived and thrived in order to benefit someone else, to multiply the blessings.

It is as if we are putting puzzles together and you have all of these 500-piece puzzles or 1000-piece puzzles, and sometimes it takes a while to get all the edges right. But as soon as we do, we can begin to fill the inside.

For us in our own lives, that is where the sweetness of life is. You have to smooth out and build your edges, build your aesthetic, the thing that people see. Once the outside is framed and outlined, we begin to work deeper on the inside to fortify and create the picture that everyone sees.

FINAL REMINDERS:

1. You have everything it takes to bounce back right inside of you. Lean in and tap into your own resources, and

all you have to offer, not only for yourself, but for others.

2. The unique situations and stories you experience create compelling, redemptive stories that are not only for you, but to be a catalyst for change in the lives of others. Don't just share your testimony, own it with pride. You're awesome and can (and will!) enact change.

3. You're not alone. Even in the darkest of night, God is with you. He promises to never to leave you, nor forsake you.

4. Acknowledge your feelings instead of burying them. Cry if you must, slow down, but don't ever stay in that place for too long. Keep moving forward.

5. Adopt a positive mindset and begin to cultivate a spirit of gratitude. Your whole perspective will change, even amidst the hardships, when you begin to count your blessings.

6. Asking for help is not a sign of weakness; neither is accepting it if it is offered.

7. Take on a positive mindset. Begin, or continue in, affirming yourself. You are stronger today than you were yesterday.

8. Learn from the mistakes made; go forward wiser and work smarter. Don't be afraid to shake off the old even if it means walking away from family and friends. Not everyone will see you and your journey to the end.

9. Make yourself a priority. Self-care is a must. You can't pour from an empty cup, so you have to refuel and rejuvenate regularly. Make sure that you invest in yourself and continue your growth process. Setting boundaries doesn't make you a bad person, it makes you a healthy person.

10. Make a plan. While you don't know what is going to happen in the future, you can always plan ahead. Look at the patterns in your life and see what challenges you are struggling with. Assess the optimal outcomes and make a plan for how you can achieve them.

www.ingramcontent.com/pod-product-compliance
Lightning Source LLC
Chambersburg PA
CBHW070124100426
42744CB00010B/1913